HIGH-OCTANE CAREERS

VOLCANOLOGIST

BY THEIA LAKE

HOT TOPICS

Gareth Stevens PUBLISHING

Please visit our website, www.garethstevens.com. For a free color catalog of all our high-quality books, call toll free 1-800-542-2595 or fax 1-877-542-2596.

Cataloging-in-Publication Data

Names: Lake, Theia.
Title: Volcanologist / Theia Lake.
Description: Buffalo, NY : Gareth Stevens Publishing, 2025. | Series: High-octane careers | Includes glossary.
Identifiers: ISBN 9781482469325 (pbk.) | ISBN 9781482469332 (library bound) | ISBN 9781482469349 (ebook)
Subjects: LCSH: Volcanologists–Juvenile literature. | Volcanological research–Juvenile literature. | Geology–Vocational guidance–Juvenile literature. | Volcanoes–Juvenile literature.
Classification: LCC QE34.L25 2025 | DDC 551.21023–dc23

Published in 2025 by
Gareth Stevens Publishing
2544 Clinton Street
Buffalo, NY 14224

Designer: Claire Zimmermann
Editor: Theresa Emminizer

Photo credits: Cover, p. 1 (woman) AnnaTamila/Shutterstock.com; cover, p.1 (volcano background) Sandra Sev Jarocka/Shutterstock.com; cover, p. 1 (lower magma photo) Artistic_Edge/Shutterstock.com; cover, p.1 (series title light flare) SpicyTruffel/Shutterstock.com; series art (background texture) Golubovy/Shutterstock.com; p. 5 Dimitri Tymchenko/Shutterstock.com; p. 7 Thorir Ingvarsson/Shutterstock.com; p. 9 Yvonne Baur/Shutterstock.com; p. 11 Strahil Dimitrov/Shutterstock.com; p. 13 Evgeny Haritonov/Shutterstock.com; p. 15 Kirill Chernyshev/Shutterstock.com; p. 17 Iv-olga/Shutterstock.com; p. 19 Aldha Aulia Pangestu/Shutterstock.com; p. 21 Tyler Olson/Shutterstock.com; p. 23 Maksym Kaharlyk/Shutterstock.com; p. 25 California Volcano Observatory operations room.jpg/Wikimedia Commons; p. 27 Fishman64/Shutterstock.com; p. 29 Lapina/Shutterstock.com; p. 30 (icons) Parbat Devkota/Shutterstock.com.

Printed in the United States of America

CONTENTS

A BIG BLAST!

BOOM! A great blast shakes the ground! Dark smoke fills the sky! Glowing **liquid** flows down. It's a volcanic eruption! A volcano is an opening in Earth's crust. When it erupts, or blows up, hot, liquid rock called magma flows out. Volcanologists study volcanoes!

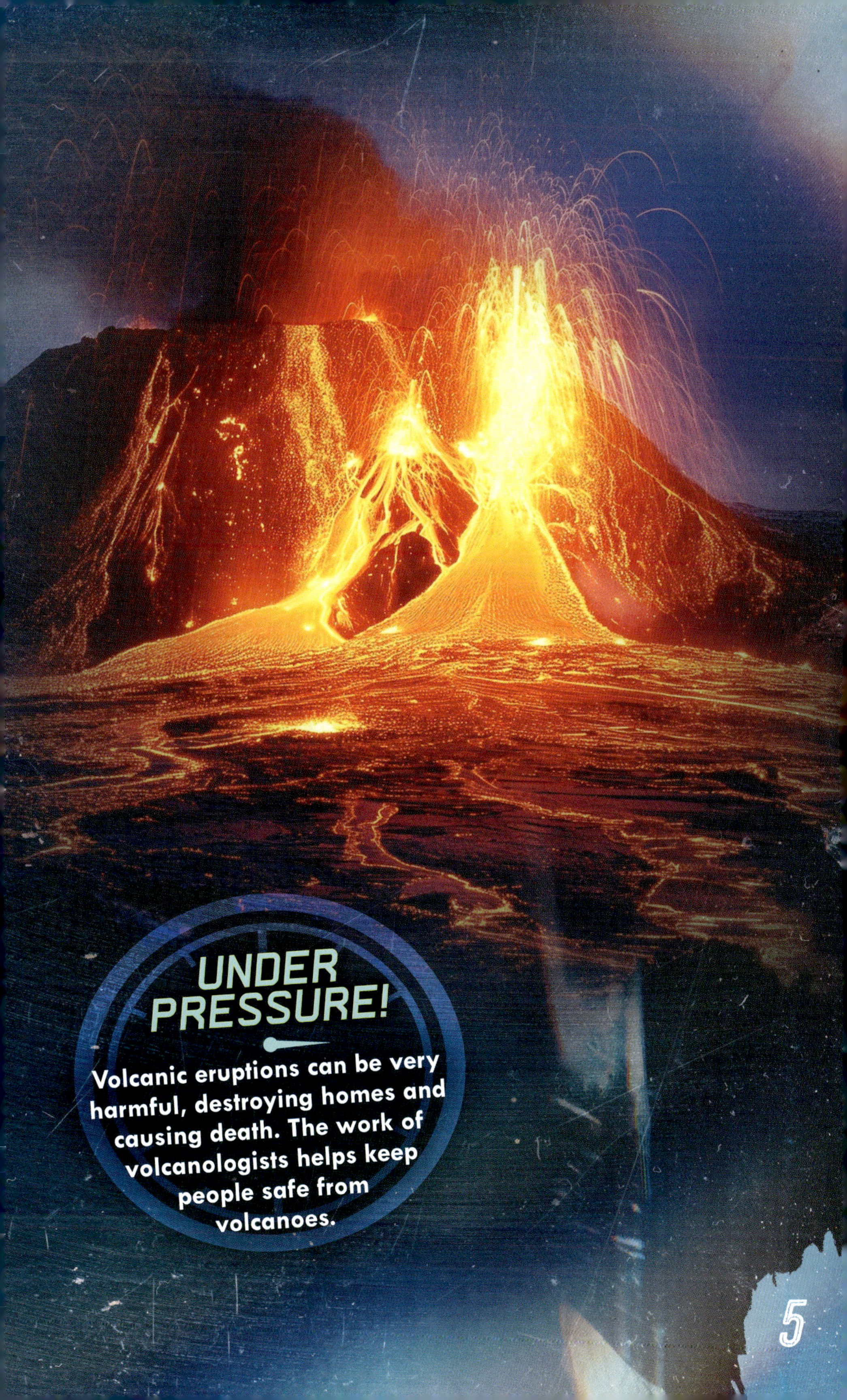

UNDER PRESSURE!

Volcanic eruptions can be very harmful, destroying homes and causing death. The work of volcanologists helps keep people safe from volcanoes.

A VOLCANOLOGIST'S JOB

Volcanologists study how volcanoes form, what they're made of, and how they act. They also study how volcanoes affect the environment, or natural world around them. They find out what kind of harm volcanoes can cause and help make plans to keep communities safe.

UNDER PRESSURE!

Volcanoes can be found all over the world. Millions of people live near them. Volcanic eruptions can cause other **natural disasters** such as landslides and earthquakes.

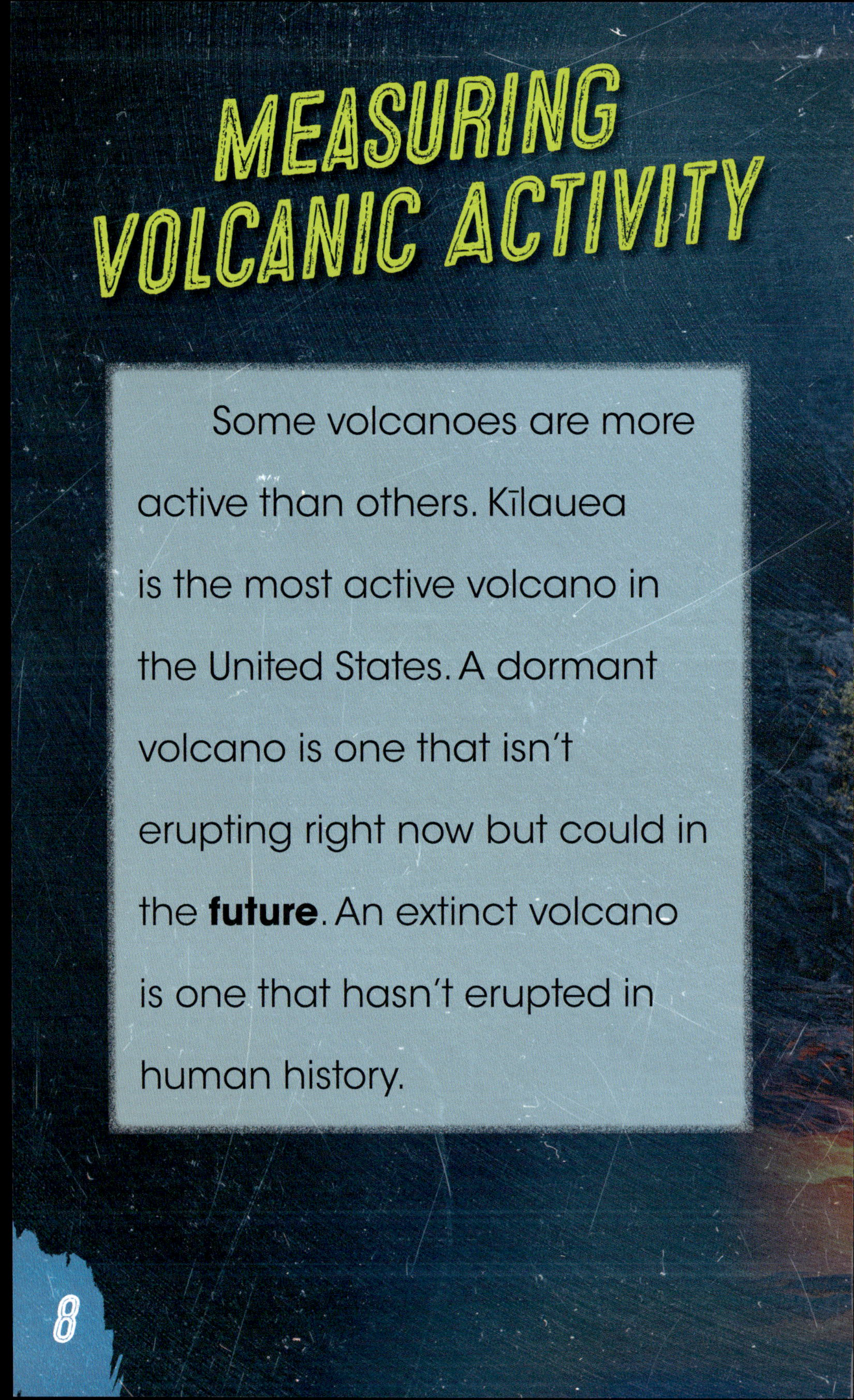

MEASURING VOLCANIC ACTIVITY

Some volcanoes are more active than others. Kīlauea is the most active volcano in the United States. A dormant volcano is one that isn't erupting right now but could in the **future**. An extinct volcano is one that hasn't erupted in human history.

UNDER PRESSURE!

When magma reaches Earth's surface it's called lava. Lava can be as hot as 2,200°F (1,204°C)!

MONITORING ACTIVITY

Volcanologists closely monitor, or watch, volcanic activity. They use special equipment, or tools, to track the gases being emitted, or let out, from the volcano. Some equipment tracks seismic activity, which is vibrations, or tiny movements, in Earth and its crust.

UNDER PRESSURE!

Volcanologists set up equipment at volcanic sites so that they can monitor activity remotely, or from afar. NASA also uses **satellites** to monitor volcanic activity from space!

FIELDWORK

When volcanologists work at volcanic sites it's called fieldwork. Volcanologists do fieldwork to gather **samples** and data, or facts. Often, fieldwork is dangerous, or unsafe. Volcanologists must hike and climb up volcanoes carrying equipment and wearing special clothing and masks.

UNDER PRESSURE!

In the United States, volcanologists may do fieldwork at active volcano sites such as Kīlauea in Hawaii, Mount St. Helens in Alaska, or the Cascades in Washington, Oregon, and Northern California.

LAB WORK

Once fieldwork is complete, volcanologists bring the samples of volcanic rock, gas, and other materials they gathered back to the **laboratory**. Researching, or studying, these samples helps volcanologists understand volcanic **processes**. Knowing more about how volcanoes work could help scientists use their power for good.

UNDER PRESSURE!

Geothermal power is a form of energy made from heat within Earth. Active volcanoes are hotspots where geothermal power can be harnessed, or tapped into and used.

PUBLIC SAFETY

Volcanologists set up ways to warn, or let people know, that a volcanic eruption may be coming. Volcanologists help community leaders come up with a plan of action to evacuate people, or move them to safety, as early as they're able.

UNDER PRESSURE!

There are 169 volcanoes in the United States that may be active. Early warnings and evacuations are very important. Volcanic ash can make people very sick.

STARTING OUT

How does someone become a volcanologist? First, they need to earn a bachelor's (four-year) **degree** in a field such as geology or Earth science. Then, they need a master's degree in volcanology. Having a doctorate degree, or Ph.D., is thought to be best.

UNDER PRESSURE!

Geology is the science that studies the history of Earth and its life as recorded, or shown, in rocks. The work of geologists and volcanologists is closely linked.

GAINING EXPERIENCE

While going to school, volcanology students can gain hands-on experience by taking part in research projects and doing internships. An internship is a short-term job in which a beginner can learn from a **professional**. Students can also work as assistants, or helpers, in laboratories.

UNDER PRESSURE!

Doing internships and research projects can help volcanology students make connections within their field. Scientists work closely together, sharing their research to find answers.

SPECIAL SKILLS

In addition to being well-educated and having hands-on experience, volcanologists need certain skills to help them do their job well. Having strong math and computer skills is helpful in their work. Volcanologists must also be curious. They must think deeply about their findings.

UNDER PRESSURE!

Volcanologists also need strong bodies. Fieldwork is often unsafe and hard to get to. Volcanologists must be able to climb and work for hours at a time.

KINDS OF VOLCANOLOGISTS

There are different kinds of volcanologists. Some volcanologists focus on one part of volcanic activity, such as seismic activity. Some spend a lifetime studying just one volcano! Others travel to many different volcanic sites. Some volcanologists work for the government. Others are teachers.

UNDER PRESSURE!

A volcano observatory is a place where scientists monitor active volcanoes. There are five volcano observatories in the United States.

LIFESTYLE AND SALARY

Salary is the amount of money someone is paid for doing a job. The median, or middle, salary for geoscience jobs is around $92,580 per year. That means about half of the people who practice geoscience earn more than that, and half earn less.

UNDER PRESSURE!

Most geoscientists like volcanologists work full-time, meaning they work about 40 hours per week. When doing fieldwork, they may work longer.

WANT TO BE A VOLCANOLOGIST?

Does studying volcanoes sound exciting to you? Maybe you have what it takes to be a volcanologist! Studying geology and other Earth sciences is a great way to get started. You could also join a science club or check out books about volcanoes from your library.

UNDER PRESSURE!

Try making your own volcano! Use salt dough to make a mountain, then place a mixture of baking soda, dish soap, and vinegar inside to make it erupt!

WORST ERUPTIONS IN U.S. HISTORY

1912
NOVARUPTA, ALASKA

the largest eruption of the 20th century

May 22, 1915
LASSEN PEAK, CALIFORNIA

rained volcanic ash 200 miles (300 km) east

May 1924
KĪLAUEA, HAWAII

most deaths caused by falling rock

May 18, 1980
MOUNT ST. HELENS, WASHINGTON

most deaths caused by volcanic ash

FOR MORE INFORMATION

BOOKS

Borgert-Spaniol, Megan. *STEM Underground.* Minneapolis, MN: Checkerboard Library, an imprint of Abdo Publishing, 2024.

Van Rose, Susanna. *Eyewitness Volcano & Earthquake.* New York, NY: DK Publishing, 2022.

WEBSITES

NASA Science Space Place
spaceplace.nasa.gov/volcanoes2/en/
Find out where else volcanoes can be found in our solar system.

National Geographic Kids
www.natgeokids.com/uk/discover/geography/physical-geography/volcano-facts/
Learn more awesome facts about volcanoes!

Publisher's note to educators and parents: Our editors have carefully reviewed these websites to ensure that they are suitable for students. Many websites change frequently, however, and we cannot guarantee that a site's future contents will continue to meet our high standards of quality and educational value. Be advised that students should be closely supervised whenever they access the internet.

GLOSSARY

degree: An official paper given to someone who has completed certain classes at a college or university.

future: Time to come.

laboratory: A place with tools to perform experiments.

liquid: Something that flows and takes the shape of the container holding it.

natural disaster: A harmful event caused by the forces of nature that may result in loss of life, injury, and damage to property.

process: A series of steps or actions taken to complete something.

professional: Having to do with a job someone does for a living.

sample: A small amount of something gathered in order to be studied by scientists.

satellite: An object that circles Earth in order to collect and send information or aid in communication.

INDEX